BANGKOK

HORIZON

Bangkok Horizon - A new vision of the City of Angels

First published 2013
Copyright © 2013

Li-Zenn Publishing Limited

Publisher :	Nithi Sthapitanonda	Editor:	Nithi Sthapitanonda
Managing Director :	Suluck Visavapattamawon	Managing Editor:	Pisut Lertdumrikarn
Deputy Managing Director :	Pisut Lertdumrikarn	Graphic Designer:	Srirath Somsawat
Executive Director :	Prabhakorn Vadanyakul	Editorial Assistant:	Jutarut Wongthai
	Kiattisak Veteewootacharn		Rungkit Charoenwat
		Translator:	Jutamas Tadthiemrom (p.6, p.104)
		English Editing:	Ruairi Cunningham

81 Sukhumvit 26, Klongton, Klongtoey, Bangkok 10110 Thailand
T: +66 (0) 2259 2096, F: +66 (0) 2661 2017
li-zenn@li-zenn.com, www.li-zenn.com

Distributor :   Li-Zenn Publishing Limited
                  81 Sukhumvit 26, Klongton, Klongtoey,
                  Bangkok 10110 Thailand
                  T: +66 (0) 2259 2096, F: +66 (0) 2661 2017
                  li-zenn@li-zenn.com, www.li-zenn.com

National Library of Thailand Cataloging in Publication Data
Srirath Somsawat .
   Bangkok Horizon .– Bangkok : Li-Zenn, 2013.
   104 p.

   1. Photographs. 2. Bangkok–Photographs.   I. Title.

779
ISBN: 978-616-7800-23-3

Printed in China by Tiger Printing (Hong Kong)

Front cover: Bangkok view from Krungthep Bridge
Back cover: Wat Prathumwanaram, Wat Ratchanaddaram, Wat Phrachetuphon, Khaosan Raod, Wat Arun, Aerial View of Bangkok, Lumpinee Park & the Erawan Shrine

A NEW VISION OF THE CITY OF ANGELS

BANGKOK

HORIZON

PHOTOGRAPHY: **SRIRATH SOMSAWAT**

Li-Zenn

Bangkok, Thailand's capital city, has earned its reputation as one of the best and most tourist friendly cities in the world. 'Venice of the East' is used as the second name for Bangkok as the city is full of rivers and canals and the locals have relied on these waterways along the both sides of the banks for hundreds of years. Furthermore, The Chao Phraya River, the main river of the city is the location for significant landmarks including the Grand Palace which is situated in the center of Ko Rattanakosin, the heart of Thai people and the heart of governance in the past.

However, the traces of more than 200 years of prosperity remain in the traditional style of architecture until the arrival of the western influence and the role of rivers has been discrete. The significant landmarks which have changed the face of Bangkok are the concrete buildings along Ratchadamnern Avenue where the style is inspired by The Avenue des Champs-Élysées in Paris. The journey of styles has never stopped, Bangkok has followed the world movement and opened itself to the new trends of architecture including metal, glass, and digital screens and used them as part of the urban development.

From the heart of the city at Rattanakosin Island, Bangkok has expanded to the nearby areas of Charoenkrung, Silom, and to the other side of town in Sukhumvit. Bangkok has sparked a taste revolution and become the metropolis of opportunities, the economic centre of Thailand and ASEAN. Nevertheless, the distinctiveness of traditional culture and lifestyle exist in every inch of the city and this diversity has made Bangkok an astounding and charming city for tourists to visit.

Bangkok Horizon is one of the memorial photo books or souvenir books which generally combine the collection of top attraction sites and city atmosphere except that most pictures that have been taken for this book are in panorama which required a tremendous effort in discovering the perfect wide angle to capture the entire city sphere as well as spending time waiting for the right moments of lights, shadows, and live movements in order to unfold the best city story that has ever been told. This is the book, Li-zenn Publishing proudly presents to readers not only as a publishing house but also as a host who takes part in welcoming visitors to return home with unforgettable memories of Bangkok, which is known in Thai as Krungthep - **the City of Angels**.

The Grand Palace (Phra Borom Maha Ratchawang)
Residence and administrative center of the King of
Siam since 17th century

View from the Vises Chaisri Gate,
main entrance of The Grand Palace

Temple of the Emerald Buddha (Wat Phra Kaew or Wat Phra Si Rattana Sassadaram) the most sacred Buddhist temple in Thailand

The Bangkok National Museum, the old palace o
the second king (front palace or Wang Na) since
the King Rama I era, houses the exhibition of Tha
History, dated from Dvaravati, Srivijaya up to
Sukhothai, Ayutthaya and Rattanakosin period

The beautiful panoramic scene inside the Buddhaisawan Throne Hall at The Bangkok National Museum

Temple of the Reclining Buddha (Wat Pho or Wat Phra Chetuphon Wimol Mangklaram) One of the oldest temples in Bangkok which has been registered as Memory World in 2011 by UNESCO

Week day water transportation in the Chao Phraya River

Temple of Dawn (Wat Arun Ratchawararam)
located on the other side of the Chao Phraya
River, opposite Nagaraphirom, the public
park near the Temple of the Reclining Buddha

The Temple of dawn, a good view point of the old historic
area of Ko Rattanakosin to downtown Bangkok

Collections of glory Thai Arts and Culture in Ko Rattanakosin: (from left to right and clockwise) Rattanakosin Exhibition Hall, the Kin Rama V Memorial Exhibition, Silpa Bhirasri National Museum, Museum Siam, The National Gallery Bangkok Chao Fa Road, Hal of Sculpture at the Fine Art Department, and (next page) National Museum of Royal Barges.

Bangkok temple's tourist attractions:
(this page) Wat Ratchabophit, by the unique lay
out and the western style of interior decoration
(next page) Wat Suthat Thep Wararam, togethe
with the Giant Swing in front

The Giant Swing and Wat Suthat area by night, in this area there are a lot of Buddhism statue shops in every size, every style and every material: bronze, brass or fiberglass

The popular Khao Sarn Road, residence, shopping or even eating, everything that you can imagine for tourist live 24 hours a day

Santi Chai Prakarn Park and the Phra Sumen fort
Opportunities for people to appreciate the
atmosphere along the Chao Phraya River and
Rama VIII Bridge

Wat Bowonniwet Vihara
A major temple of patronage for the Chakri
dynasty and scene of the most beautiful Buddha
image called Phra Buddha Shin Si

King Rama III Memorial Park (Maha Jessada Bodin
Courtyard Pavillion) on Ratchadamnern Avenue

The Metal Castle (Loha Prasat) at Wat Ratchanaddaram
Unique architectural style, it was 1 of 3 places in the world but the only one remaining of its kind

(next page) Wat Ratchanaddaram and Wat Saket Ratcha Wora Maha Wihan view from the view point of the Rattanakosin Exhibition Hall

Phra Borom Bunpot (Phu Kaho Thong or the Golden Mount) at Wat Saket Ratcha Wora Maha Wihan, walk up 344 steps to the Golden Pagoda, a 360 degree view point of Ko Rattanakosin.

Aerial view of Ko Rattanakosin on December 5th, the King Bhumibol's birthday, in the scene: Wat Ratchanadda, Wat Suthat and the Giant Swing, Democracy Monument, The Grand Palace and at the far left Wat Arun

Dusk at Ratchadamnern Avenue, back and forth
view from the Panfa Leelas Bridge

The Ananta Samakhom
Neo Renaissance architectural style, was ordered by King
Rama V to be the Throne Hall

(next page) Parade of Thais on worship ceremony for
their Great Beloved King (Phra Piya Maharat), or King
Rama V in front of the King Rama V statue, in front of The
Ananta Samakhomthrone Hall every year

The Marble temple (Wat Benchamabophit Dusitvanaram)
One of Bangkok's most beautiful temples w perfect proportion and details of material

Another influence from the west which is still seen today
The Abhisek Dusit Throne Hall (this page), part of Dusit Palace and Phayathai
Palace (next page), the Art Culture and Architectural museum

Lao Pun Tao Kong Shrine and the Chinese lifestyle
At Yaowarat Area, the China town of Bangkok

Thai and Chinese culture mixed up
The Yaowarat Heritage Museum at the Golden
Buddha Temple, the biggest golden Buddhist
statue in the world (Wat Traimit Widayaram)

Time out at Bangkok Railway Station (Hua Lum Phong) the main railway station of Bangkok

The Memorial Bridge (Phra Buddha Yodfa Bridge)
Across the Chao Phraya River, the Royal Monument of King Rama I the Great is located,

The Princess Mother Memorial Park (Suan Somdet Ya)
Sit back and relax in this homely public space and community level, located on Klong San
area, a few minutes' walk from Ko Rattanakosin across the Chao Phraya River.

Chao Phraya River (Mae Nam Chao Phraya)
Defines Bangkok into 2 parts and creates plen
business along her length of 372 kilometres

Bang Rak and Sathorn, the down town of Bangkok view from the Krungthep Bridge

Silom Road is one of Bangkok's
once was called the Wall Street
Sathorn Road

Just across the street from the Silom area, there is the 360-acre Lumpinee Park, Bangkok's first public park since 1925

Group of modern buildings on Ratchaprasong and Wireless (Wittayu) Road has set the Bangkok skyline

(next page) Little green area of the Royal Bangkok Sport Club under the shadow of the giant concrete blocks at the Ratchaprasong area

ew from the tallest building in Thailand, The Bai Yoke Tower 2,
a height of 305 metres

Shopaholic center, from Ratchaprasong to Pathumwan Intersection although there are about 10 shopping heavens along this area but 8 shrines of the Hindu goddess and 1 one half century-old temple (Wat Pathum Wanaram) appear, showing that spirituality is a big influence in Thai beliefs

Modernized culture, knowledge and creativity always set for new generation by Siam Center and Bangkok Art and Culture Centre

The famous MBK Center and Jim Thomson House Museum, the famous museum of Art , architecture and textiles especially Thai Silk, the old house of the American entrepreneur, sit on the same Rama I road

An aerial view of Northern Bangkok and its destination,
The Museum of Contemporary Art (MOCA) the museum
of the Thai traditional to contemporary Art by Thai Artists

Wachira Benchatat Park, Queen Sirikit Park and Chatuchak Park
Those three parks contain a total of 375 acres of lush green trees, where Chatuchak Weekend Market is the closest neighbor

Sukhumvit area
Bangkok's newest business district, home for the expats

(next page) Bangkok's Sukhumvit skyline view from
Benjakitti Park

Many modern skyscrapers that make Bangkok 1 of 25 the world tallest cities

Up above, there is the BTS Skytrain running along to
Chatuchak Park

Sky discoloration, dramatic views of downtown Bangkok

Long lasting night on Sukhumvit and Silom road in the background

The beautiful construction line and curve of the Industrial Ring Road Bridge, the official name is
Bhumibol Bridge, named after the current, and long standing King of Thailand

Miraculous scene inside the tummy of the three-headed elephant at Erawan Museum (Airavata), another attraction at Samut Prakan province

Mythology of God Vishnu on believing will create prosperity of the infinite sculpture at
Suvarnabhumi International Airport

BANGKOK HORIZON

Srirath Somsawat
www.aey.me

Started taking architectural photography as a hobby in the 80's
based on his view as an architect. His style of photography
aimed to present lifestyle within the context of places. As time
passed, Srirath-aey has gained more experience and learned
more, he realized that these types of images are not popular
in Thailand. Srirath then turned to shoot photographs related to
architecture, especially in Bangkok where he was born and lives.
When opportunities arrive, he wastes no time in combining and
putting words to describe the pictures until it eventually becomes
Bangkok Horizon - A new vision of the City of Angels in your
hands.